S0-CPC-308

Alfred's
Premier Piano Course

Edited by Gayle Kowalchyk • E. L. Lancaster

Alfred's *Premier Piano Course: Duet Book 6* includes motivational music that reinforces concepts introduced in Lesson Book 6. The duets for one piano, four hands continue the strong pedagogical focus of the course while providing the enjoyment of playing with a friend or family member.

The pieces in this book correlate page by page with the materials in Lesson Book 6. They should be assigned according to the instructions in the upper right corner of selected pages of this book. They also may be assigned as review material at any time after the student has passed the designated Lesson Book page.

Written by America's leading pedagogical composers, these duets contain equally leveled parts for *primo* and *secondo*. Within each duet, melodic material is shared between the parts. A variety of moods, styles, and forms are featured, including jazz, ragtime, pieces in Romantic and Contemporary styles, and an arrangement of the famous *Canon in D* of Johann Pachelbel.

Duets provide social opportunities for students, especially those who practice solo repertoire most of the time. Teachers recognize the importance of piano duets in developing musicianship, ensemble performance skills, sight-reading ability, musical understanding, rhythmic awareness, and listening skills.

These duets can be used as supplementary material for any course of piano study. They are motivating repertoire selections for group lessons and ensemble classes. Students will enjoy performing these pieces on recitals, "monster" concerts, or for other special occasions.

Contents

ISBN-10: 1-4706-2648-9
ISBN-13: 978-1-4706-2648-8

Use with Alfred's Premier Piano Course
Lesson Book 6, pages 6–7.

Changing Times

Secondo

Robert D. Vandall

Changing Times

Primo

Robert D. Vandall

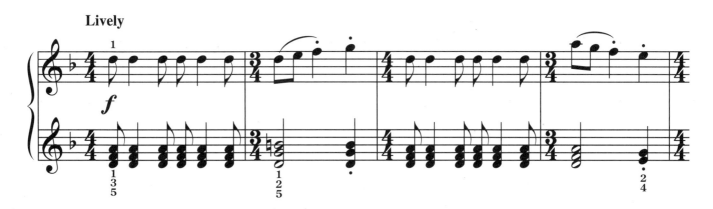

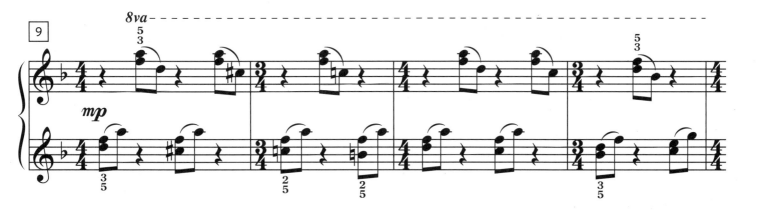

Secondo

Lesson Book: pages 10–11

Reflections in the Waves

Secondo

Mike Springer

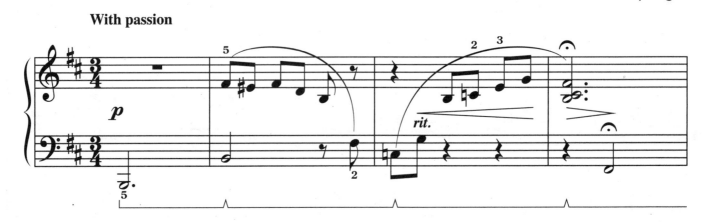

Reflections in the Waves

Primo

Mike Springer

Secondo

Primo

Secondo

Lesson Book: pages 16–17

The Great Expanse

Secondo

Tom Gerou

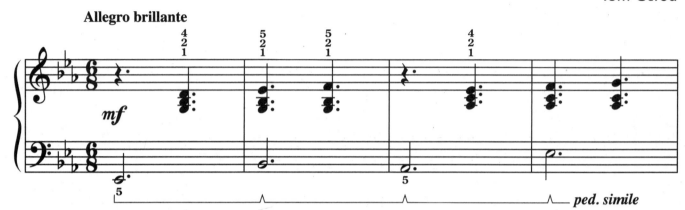

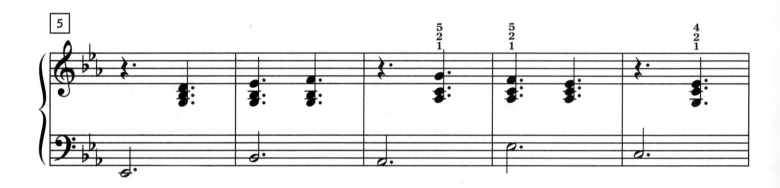

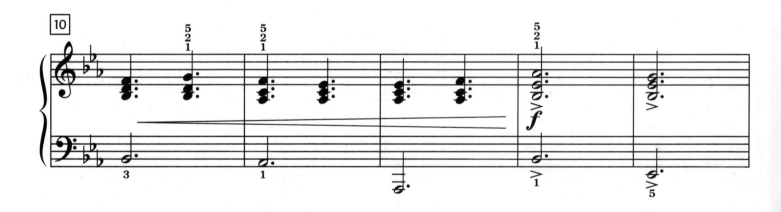

The Great Expanse

Primo

Tom Gerou

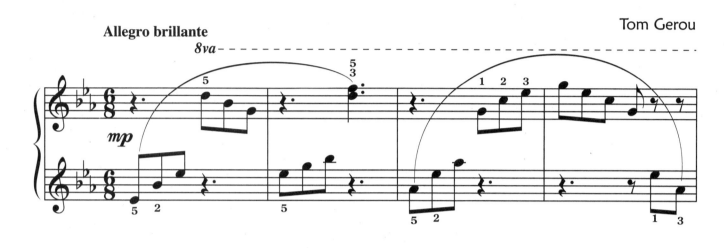

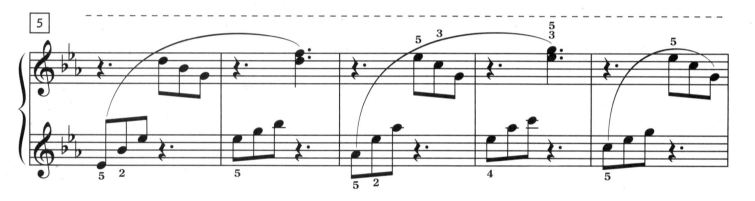

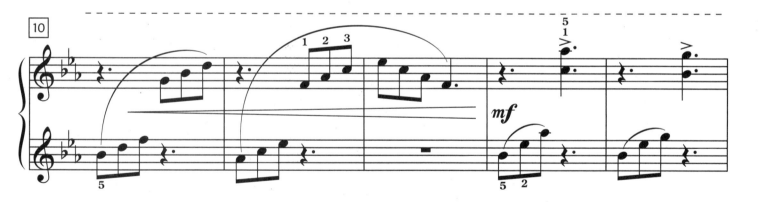

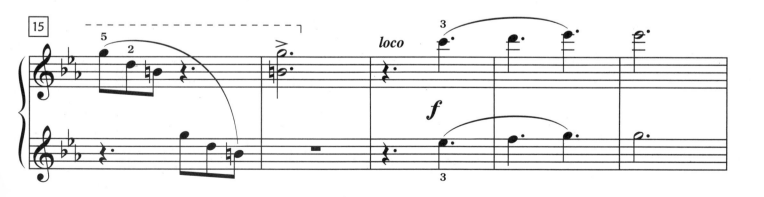

Secondo

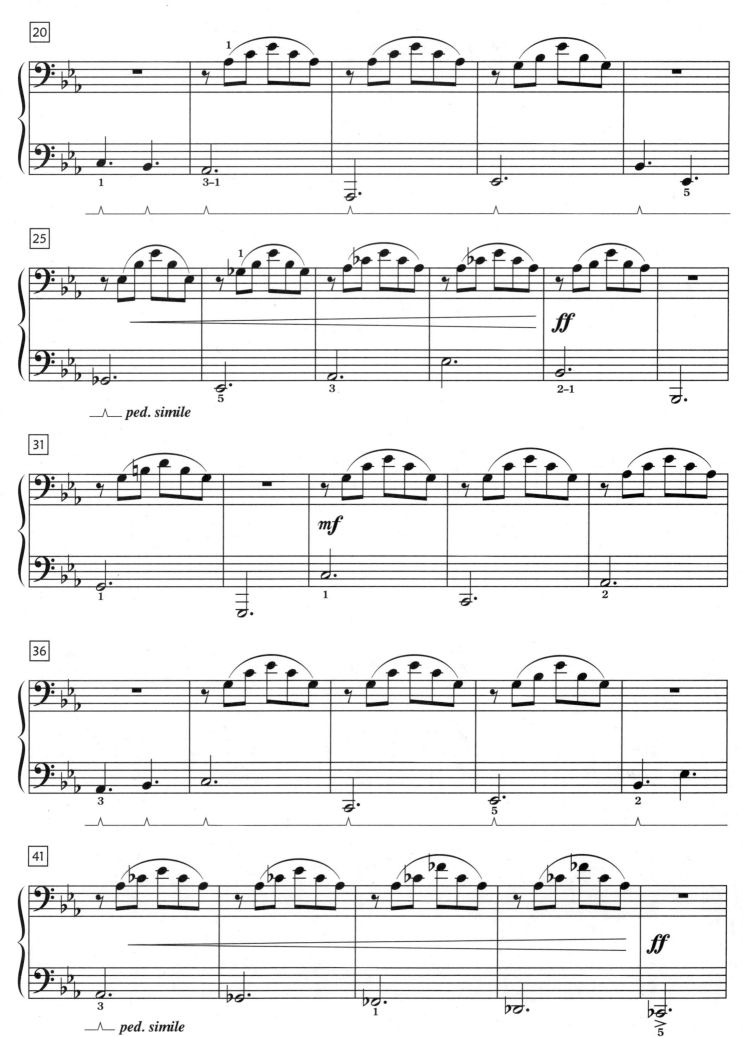

Primo

Secondo

Lesson Book: pages 26–27

Romance in A-flat Major

Secondo

Dennis Alexander

Romance in A-flat Major

Primo

Dennis Alexander

Cantabile e molto espressivo

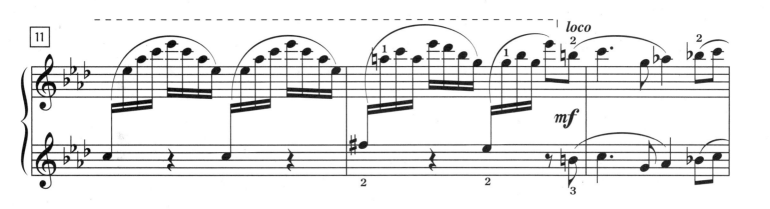

Secondo

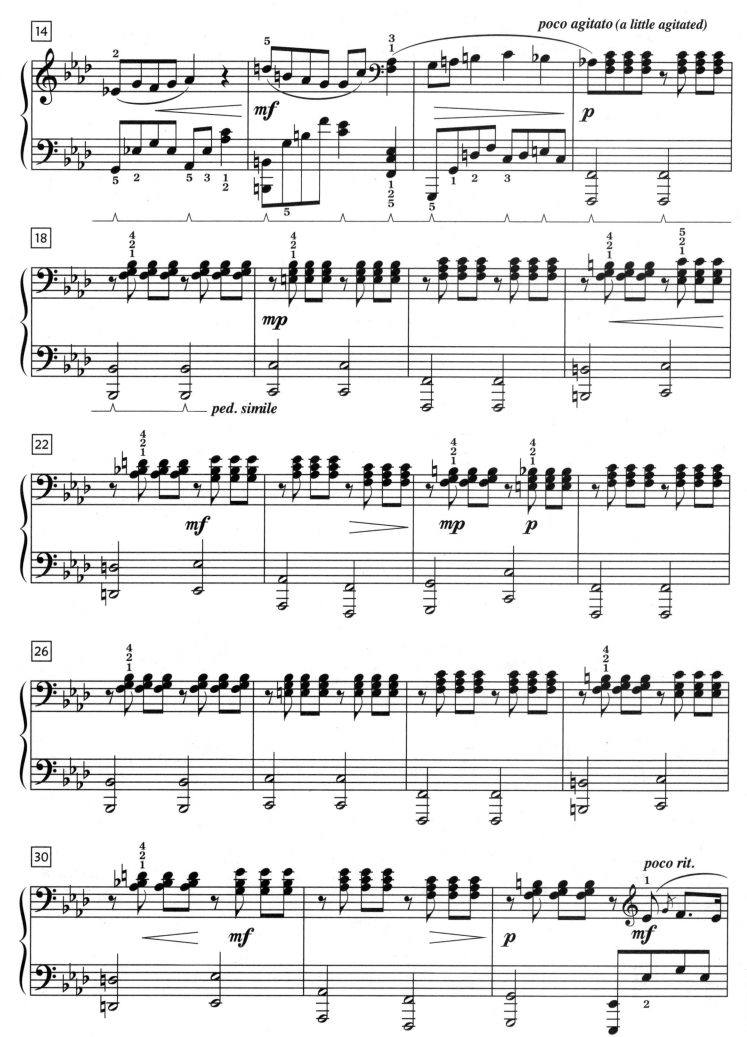

Primo

Secondo

Primo

Lesson Book: page 29

Baltic Dance

Secondo

Wynn-Anne Rossi

Baltic Dance

Primo

Wynn-Anne Rossi

Secondo

Primo

Lesson Book: pages 31–33

Canon in D

Secondo

Johann Pachelbel (1653–1706)
Arr. Carol Matz

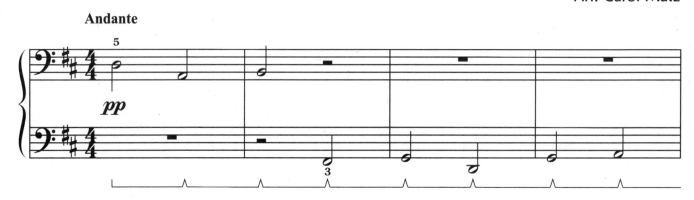

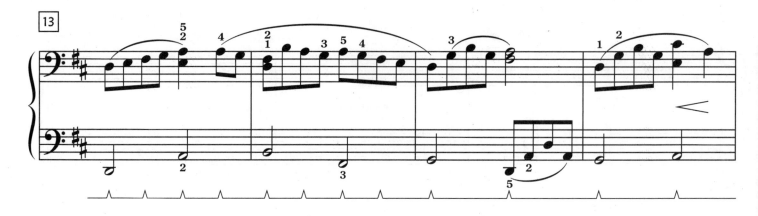

Canon in D

Primo

Johann Pachelbel (1653–1706)
Arr. Carol Matz

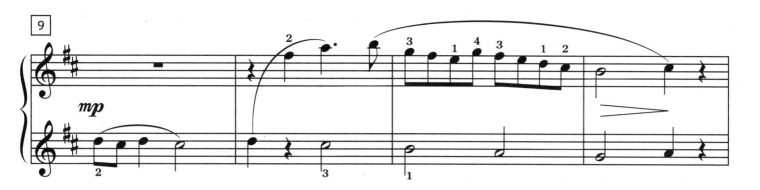

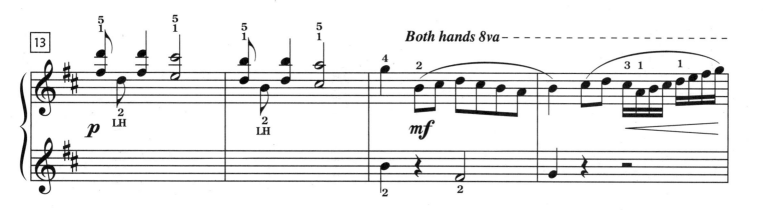

Secondo

Primo

Lesson Book: pages 41–43

Friday Night Jazz

Secondo

Melody Bober

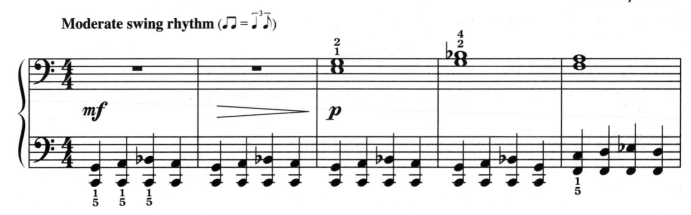

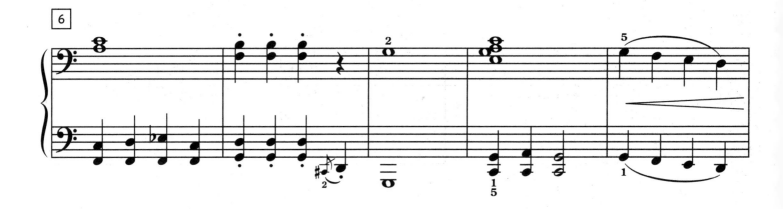

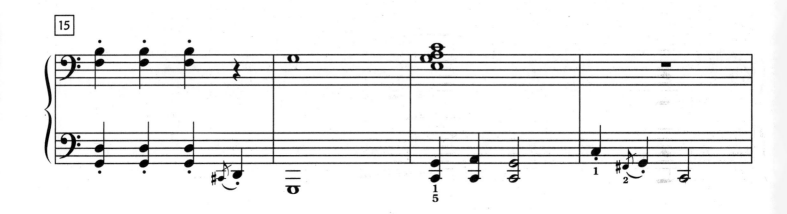

Friday Night Jazz

Primo

Melody Bober

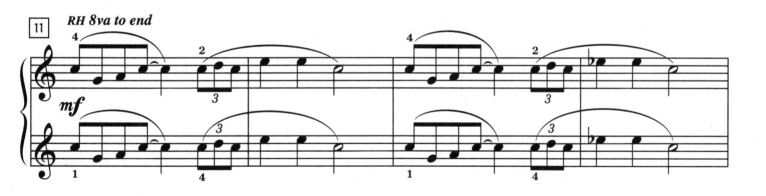

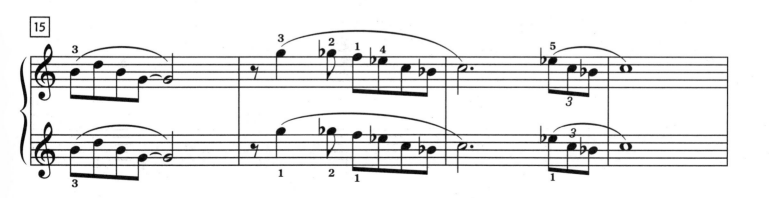

Secondo

Primo

Lesson Book: pages 54–55

Wildflower Rag

Secondo

Martha Mier

Wildflower Rag

Primo

Martha Mier

Secondo

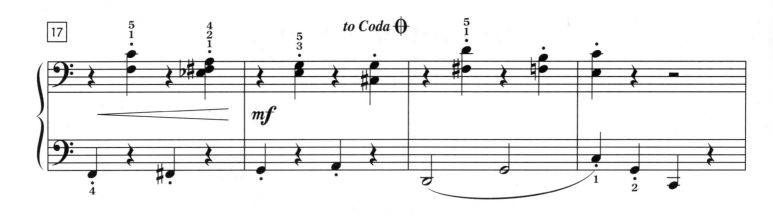

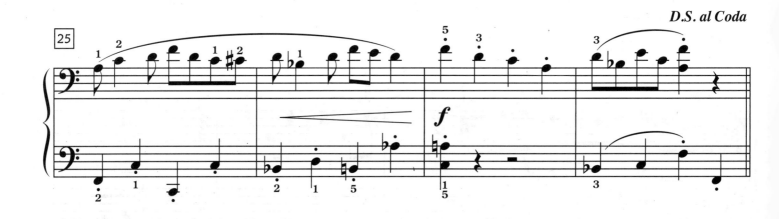

Primo

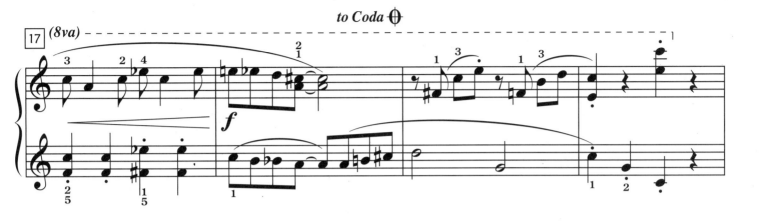

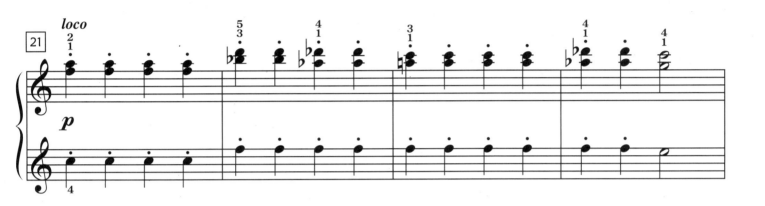

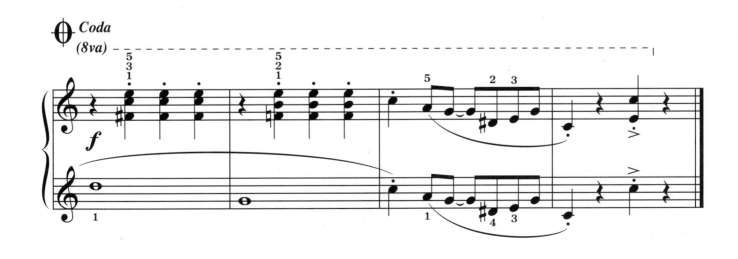